NATURE'S CHILDREN

ALLIGATORS

by Timothy M. Daly

Children's Press®

An Imprint of Scholastic Inc.
New York Toronto London Auckland Sydney
Mexico City New Delhi Hong Kong
Danbury, Connecticut

Content Consultant
Dr. Stephen S. Ditchkoff
Professor of Wildlife Sciences
Auburn University
Auburn, Alabama

Library of Congress Cataloging-in-Publication Data

Daly, Timothy M.
   Alligators/by Timothy M. Daly.
      p. cm.—(Nature's children)
   Includes bibliographical references and index.
   ISBN 978-0-531-20975-2 (library binding)
   ISBN 978-0-531-24301-5 (pbk.)
1. Alligators—Juvenile literature. I. Title.
   QL666.C925D35 2013
   597.98'4—dc23   2012030354

Alligators

Class	Reptilia
Order	Crocodylia
Family	Alligatoridae
Genus	*Alligator*
Species	*Alligator mississippiensis* (American alligator), *Alligator sinensis* (Chinese alligator)
World distribution	The American alligator is found only in the southeastern United States; the Chinese alligator is found only near the lower Yangtze River in China
Habitats	Can be found on the edges of ponds, lakes, rivers, marshlands, and swamps
Distinctive physical characteristics	Large body, usually black or dark green, with a light underside; covered in scales; four short legs and a long, muscular tail; eyes, ears, and nostrils located on upper surface of head; rounded snout; young alligators have yellow banded stripes on their bodies and tails
Habits	Mainly lives alone; active during summer months; spends time in burrows during cold weather; females bury eggs in a nest of plant matter and mud, and guard them until they hatch
Diet	Larger alligators feed mainly on large mammals; smaller ones feed mainly on fish, turtles, birds, and small mammals

Contents

CHAPTER 1

Kings of the Swamplands

In the dim evening light, a young deer makes its way toward the edge of a nearby pond. With no threats in sight, the deer feels safe enough to bend down and take a sip of the cool water. All of a sudden, an enormous pair of jaws explodes from beneath the surface of the pond and snaps shut around the deer's neck. These jaws belong to an American alligator, one of the world's most powerful predators. The deer struggles at first, but it is too late. The alligator quickly drags its meal down under the water and begins to eat.

Alligators are fearsome hunters. They occupy a comfortable position at the top of the food chain. This means that no other animal hunts them. They have thick skin covered in protective, rectangular scales, and their fierce jaws are lined with pointy teeth. Such features have made them the kings of the swamplands.

Alligators are among nature's deadliest hunters.

Happy Homes

There are two different alligator species. The biggest difference between them is where they live. The American alligator is found throughout the warm climates of the southeastern United States. Florida and Louisiana are home to the majority of these massive predators. American alligators can also be found as far north as North Carolina and as far west as central Texas and southeastern Oklahoma. They reach as far south as the southern point of Florida. The other species is the Chinese alligator. It is found only along the lower Yangtze River in China.

Both alligator species live in or near freshwater sources. Marshes, ponds, slow-moving rivers, lakes, and swamps all make excellent alligator habitats. Alligators can also survive in brackish water, which is a mixture of freshwater and saltwater. They sometimes travel into pure saltwater to hunt for food, but they only stay there for short periods of time.

Chinese alligators are much rarer than their American cousins.

Gazing at Gators

Alligators are most commonly black or dark green in color. They have thick, scaly skin. Bony plates called **scutes** cover their backs, and their bellies are a creamy white color. Wide, rounded snouts give their faces a distinctive shape. They have four short legs, with five toes on each front foot and four toes on each back one.

Male alligators are longer and heavier than females. They also grow at a faster rate than females do. An adult male American alligator is usually between 6 and 12 feet (1.8 and 3.7 meters) long and can weigh up to 1,000 pounds (454 kilograms). Adult females weigh about 250 pounds (113 kg) on average. Chinese alligators are generally smaller than their American relatives. They are usually between 4.5 and 6 feet (1.4 and 1.8 m) long and weigh around 88 pounds (40 kg).

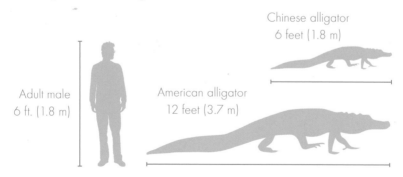

Chinese alligator
6 feet (1.8 m)

Adult male
6 ft. (1.8 m)

American alligator
12 feet (3.7 m)

An alligator's light-colored underside makes it harder for animals swimming below to see it when looking up toward the water's surface.

The Warmth of the Sun

Like all **reptiles**, alligators are cold-blooded. This means they cannot control their own body temperature. Instead, they rely on sunlight to help warm themselves when they need to raise body temperature. The dark color of their skin helps them soak up this warmth.

An alligator floats very close to the surface when it is in the water. The scutes on its back and the nostrils at the end of its snout stick out above, while the rest of its body stays hidden underwater. As a result, an alligator often looks a lot like a floating log. Since its nostrils point upward, the alligator can breathe while the scutes absorb warmth from the sun. The alligator's silvery eyes are located at the very top of its head. They also stay above the surface of the water, allowing the alligator to keep an eye out for its next meal.

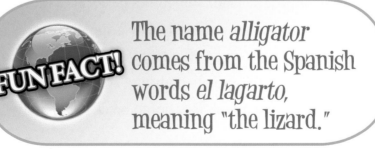

FUN FACT! The name *alligator* comes from the Spanish words *el lagarto,* meaning "the lizard."

Alligators sometimes climb out of the water to soak up sunlight when they need to warm themselves.

CHAPTER 2

Gators in the Wild

Alligators are carnivores. They feed on everything from fish, birds, and frogs to large mammals. The larger the alligator, the larger the prey it will attack.

Alligators feed mainly at night. They are not typical predators. They do not move around to hunt for food. Instead, they patiently wait for prey to come near. An alligator launches a surprise attack once an unlucky animal is close enough.

Smaller prey is captured and swallowed whole. Larger prey puts up more of a struggle. In such cases, the alligator grabs its victim and drags it underwater to drown it. When an animal is too big to swallow whole, the alligator sometimes performs a move called a death roll. It spins its body around while gripping the prey in its teeth. This allows it to twist off chunks of meat. Other times, an alligator will hide the animal's body and come back after it has begun to rot. The rotting flesh is easier to break apart and swallow.

Alligators do not chew their food before swallowing.

Beneath the Surface

An alligator uses its snout to locate food when it is underwater. The bumps on an alligator's snout are actually specialized pressure sensors. They are so sensitive that they can feel even the slightest ripple in the water. Alligators have a second set of clear eyelids under their regular ones. These eyelids allow them to see clearly while underwater.

When an alligator is below the surface, muscles in its nostrils close up. A bony "door" at the back of its mouth also closes. This is called the glottis. A closed glottis allows the alligator to swim underwater without drowning. An alligator can stay underwater up to two hours at a time if it does not expend too much energy.

An alligator's webbed feet and incredibly strong tail allow it to swim quickly through the water. For especially fast swimming, the alligator tucks its legs up close to the sides of its body and moves its tail back and forth to propel itself forward.

Plants on the surface of the water can provide alligators with extra cover to stay hidden from their prey.

On Solid Ground

On land, the alligator typically moves at a much slower pace than it does in the water. But if it finds something to eat or needs to escape a dangerous situation, the alligator can move rather quickly in short bursts. The alligator's legs are very short. This means that its body hangs low to the ground when it walks or runs on land.

When the alligator needs to move quickly, it uses what is called a high walk. When high walking, the alligator keeps its feet almost directly underneath its body. This allows the alligator to raise its heavy tail off the ground. Though the very tip still touches the ground, most of the tail's weight is held up which prevents it from dragging. On land, the tail can be used as a weapon if the alligator feels at risk. It is strong enough to break human bones in half.

Alligators raise their tails as high as possible when walking on land.

Big Bites

The American alligator has the strongest, most powerful bite of any living animal. It is so strong that it can crack through the hard protective shell of a turtle.

An alligator's jaws are lined with around 80 sharp, hollow teeth. These teeth are large and cone-shaped. There are an equal number of teeth on the top and bottom jaws. Anytime a tooth is lost or worn down, a new one grows in to take its place. An alligator can go through a total of 2,000 to 3,000 teeth over the course of its lifetime. As the alligator ages, it takes longer for new teeth to grow. Because of this, older alligators may have a harder time catching prey than younger alligators.

FUN FACT! The longest alligator on record had an estimated weight of 2,200 pounds (998 kg) and a length of just over 19 feet (5.8 m). This giant alligator was longer than an average car!

An alligator can snap its huge jaws shut with incredible force.

Lone Rangers

The average life span of a wild alligator is between 30 and 35 years. When in captivity, an alligator can live for up to 50 years. Adult alligators usually lead mostly solitary lives. They spend very little time with other alligators outside of mating season. Larger alligators are much more territorial than smaller ones are. While smaller gators are still not very social, they are more likely to live closer to one another.

Scientists have used radio transmitters to track the movements of alligators. This has helped us learn more about where these animals live and how far they travel. The research shows that male alligators have larger home ranges than females. An adult male's range might cover more than 1,000 acres (405 hectares) during mating season. Females do not move around as much because they are busy building nests and protecting their young.

Larger alligators are less likely to spend time near other alligators.

Settling In for Winter

Alligators must prepare ahead of time to survive the winter. To stay warm in the chilly weather, an alligator uses its snout and tail to burrow a tunnel into the earth along the edge of a waterway. These tunnels are known as gator holes. Gator holes are filled with water but have a pocket of air at the top. They can be as long as 65 feet (20 m).

As winter begins to set in, alligators become less active. The alligator goes into its gator hole and enters a dormant state. A dormant alligator's body systems slow down and use very little energy. Because it is not active, the alligator does not need to eat. Even when the water in its gator hole freezes solid, the alligator can survive if its nostrils are above the surface of the ice.

FUN FACT! Once an alligator is done with its gator hole, other animals move in to use it for shelter.

Alligators swim beneath the surface to find locations for their holes.

CHAPTER 3

Bringing Up Babies

Alligators are able to reproduce once they reach maturity. Males and females alike tend to reach maturity when they are about 6 feet (1.8 m) long.

Alligator mating season takes place in spring. Each April, males that are ready to mate begin trying to attract females. They use a variety of different methods to accomplish this. At night in the open water, a male alligator may roar or bellow to attract a female. Rubbing snouts, blowing bubbles, or exposing their necks can also get a female's attention. A male alligator may mate with several different females throughout the course of a single mating season. This increases his chances for successful reproduction.

Male alligators become especially territorial during mating season. They defend their home ranges from other males that might try to steal potential mates.

Alligators sometimes bite each other gently during the courtship process.

Nesting Time

After mating, a female alligator begins building a nest. Alligator nests are typically located on the shoreline. They measure around 2 to 3 feet (0.6 to 0.9 m) tall and 7 to 10 feet (2.1 to 3.0 m) wide, and are constructed out of mud and plants. The female is careful to build her nest in a location that will not flood.

A mother alligator is usually ready to lay her eggs sometime in June or July. She lays anywhere between 20 and 60 eggs in her nest, and then covers them up with additional mud and plant material. Heat from the sun and the nest itself incubates the eggs. It takes about 65 days for them to hatch.

The temperature of the nest during incubation determines whether the hatchlings will be male or female. Temperatures below 86 degrees Fahrenheit (30 degrees Celsius) produce only females. Temperatures above 93ºF (34ºC) produce only males. A mixture of males and females are born when the temperature is in between.

As the plants in an alligator's nest rot, they produce heat that warms the eggs.

Newborn Gators

A mother alligator does not sit on top of her nest during incubation. This would crush the eggs. Instead, she stays nearby to guard the nest from predators such as raccoons, opossums, skunks, and wilds pigs.

The eggs begin to hatch after 60 to 65 days of incubation. Alligator hatchlings have a hard bump on the end of their snouts called an egg tooth. They use this to break out of their shells. Hatchlings call out to their mother after cracking through their shells. She uncovers the nest using her front feet and snout. She then carries the hatchlings to the water in her mouth.

Baby alligators are quite small in comparison to their mother. They measure between 6 and 8 inches (15 and 20 centimeters) in length. They also have more brightly colored skin, with black and yellow bands running down their bodies.

Alligator eggs are only slightly larger than chicken eggs.

Dangerous Times

Most reptile species do not provide care or protection for their young. Babies are left to fend for themselves. However, baby alligators stay close to their mother in a group called a pod. They are in danger of being preyed upon by animals such as birds, bullfrogs, snakes, and fish. Alligator mothers do their best to protect their babies from any harm. However, many are still killed by predators.

Young alligators usually stay with their pod until they are one to three years old. However, they sometimes leave on their own when they are just a few months old.

Young alligators do not eat the same foods that adults do. They survive on insects, crayfish, snails, small fish, tadpoles, and frogs. Once they reach a length of 5 to 6 feet (1.5 to 1.8 m), they are big enough to attack and eat the same prey as other adult alligators.

Young alligators stay with their mothers until they are large enough to survive on their own.

CHAPTER 4

Family Ties

Alligators are grouped in the Crocodylia order. This order also includes crocodiles, caimans, and gharials. Together, these animals are known as crocodilians. They look alike and share many characteristics. This is because they have common ancestors.

The earliest crocodilian ancestors appeared on Earth around 200 million years ago. This means they have existed since dinosaurs roamed the planet. The first modern crocodilian species date back to around 80 million years ago. Crocodilians have not changed very much since then. One major difference is that the front legs of the ancient crocodilians were short and weak. Because they could not use their front legs to move quickly, they stood up and ran on their stronger back legs to make a quick getaway. Their bodies were still covered in thick scales and protected by bony plates just like scutes.

Some ancient crocodilians were much larger than today's species of crocodiles.

Crocodilian Cousins

Alligators make up just one of several crocodilian genera. All crocodilians look somewhat alike. They all have long tails and long mouths full of pointed teeth. Many people have trouble telling them apart. However, there are many differences between alligators, crocodiles, caimans, and gharials.

Crocodiles have longer, more triangular faces than alligators do. A crocodile also has four teeth on either side of its lower jaw that show when its mouth is closed. All of an alligator's teeth on the lower jaw are completely hidden when it closes its mouth. Typically, crocodiles are slightly larger than other crocodilians.

On average, caimans are much smaller than alligators. Adult males are usually around 4 to 6 feet (1.2 to 1.8 m) long. However, the largest species can grow as long as 20 feet (6 m). Caimans also have colored spots all over their bodies.

The gharial's extremely long, narrow snout sets it apart from other crocodilians. It lives only in the rivers of Nepal and northern India.

A caiman's size and skin coloring distinguish it from an alligator.

CHAPTER 5

Guarding Gators

In the late 1800s, alligators were often hunted for their skins. The creamy white undersides of their hides were used to make bags, belts, and shoes. In the 1950s, experts began to notice that the alligator was in danger of becoming extinct if hunting continued without any restrictions. Habitat loss was also a problem for alligators. Many people were clearing the lands these animals called home to make room for farms and buildings.

To save American alligators from extinction, the U.S. government listed them as endangered in 1967. This is just what the species needed to survive. By 1987, alligator populations had increased so much that the species was no longer considered endangered. However, American alligators are still considered to be threatened.

Though still considered threatened, the American alligator population has been growing over the past several decades.

Looking Forward

The future is not so bright for the Chinese alligator. This species is currently listed as critically endangered. Experts estimate that there are fewer than 200 Chinese alligators left in the wild. Habitat loss is the major reason behind the decline of the Chinese alligator population. The wetlands where they lived have been turned into farmland. Farmers do not want the alligators on their land because of the huge gator holes they dig for shelter. However, the Chinese government is working to fix this problem and protect the species from becoming extinct.

With any luck, these efforts will be successful, and the Chinese alligator will one day thrive again just as its American relatives do. Like all wild animals, they deserve to live and grow in their natural habitats. However, these remarkable predators have a long road ahead of them. Only with the help of people will they survive into the future.

Alligator farms allow people to raise alligators for meat and skin without harming wild populations.

Words to Know

ancestors (AN-ses-turz) — ancient animal species that are related to modern species

captivity (kap-TIV-i-tee) — the condition of being held or trapped by people

carnivores (KAR-nih-vorz) — animals that have meat as a regular part of their diet

climates (KLYE-mits) — the weather typical of places over a long period of time

dormant (DOR-muhnt) — inactive

endangered (en-DAYN-jurd) — at risk of becoming extinct, usually because of human activity

extinct (ik-STINGKT) — no longer found alive

genera (JEH-nuh-ruh) — groups of related plants or animals that are larger than a species but smaller than a family

habitats (HAB-uh-tats) — the places where an animal or a plant is usually found

hatchlings (HACH-lingz) — newborn alligators

home ranges (HOME RAYN-jiz) — areas of land in which animals spend most of their time

incubates (ING-kyuh-bates) — keeps eggs warm before they hatch

mammals (MAM-uhlz) — warm-blooded animals that have hair or fur and usually give birth to live young

mating (MAYT-ing) — joining together to produce babies

order (OR-duhr) — a category that groups different families of animals together according to similar traits that they share

predators (PREH-duh-turz) — animals that live by hunting other animals for food

prey (PRAY) — an animal that's hunted by another animal for food

reptiles (REP-tilez) — cold-blooded animals that usually have a backbone and scales and lay eggs

scutes (SKOOTS) — hard, protective plates on an alligator's back

species (SPEE-sheez) — one of the groups into which animals and plants of the same genus are divided

territorial (terr-uh-TOR-ee-uhl) — defensive of a certain area

threatened (THRET-uhnd) — at risk of becoming endangered

Habitat Map

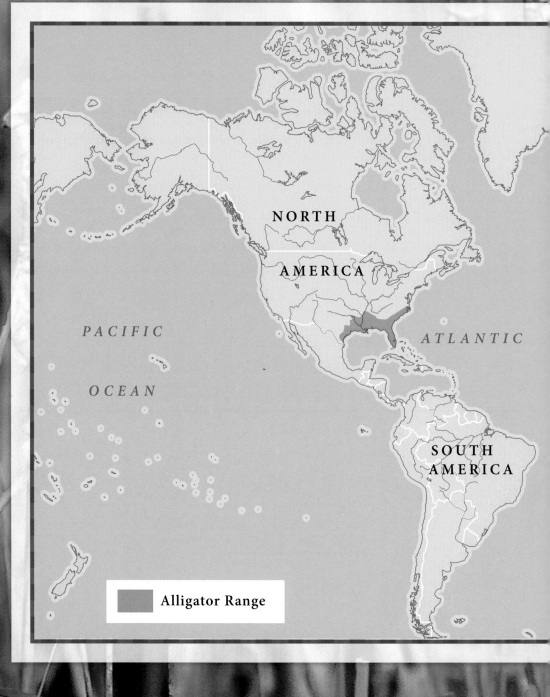

NORTH
AMERICA

SOUTH
AMERICA

PACIFIC

OCEAN

ATLANTIC

Alligator Range

ARCTIC OCEAN

EUROPE

ASIA

AFRICA

PACIFIC OCEAN

OCEAN

INDIAN

OCEAN

AUSTRALIA

Find Out More

Books

Harris, Tim, ed. *Crocodiles and Alligators*. New York: Gareth Stevens, 2010.

Haywood, Karen. *Crocodiles and Alligators*. New York: Marshall Cavendish Benchmark, 2011.

Landau, Elaine. *Alligators and Crocodiles: Hunters of the Night*. Berkeley Heights, NJ: Enslow Elementary, 2008.

Visit this Scholastic Web site for more information on alligators:
www.factsfornow.scholastic.com
Enter the keyword **Alligators**

Index

Page numbers in *italics* indicate a photograph or map.

About the Author

Timothy M. Daly studied history at Western Connecticut State University, and has lived in New England his entire life. He enjoys spending as much time as possible outside, hiking and mountain biking.